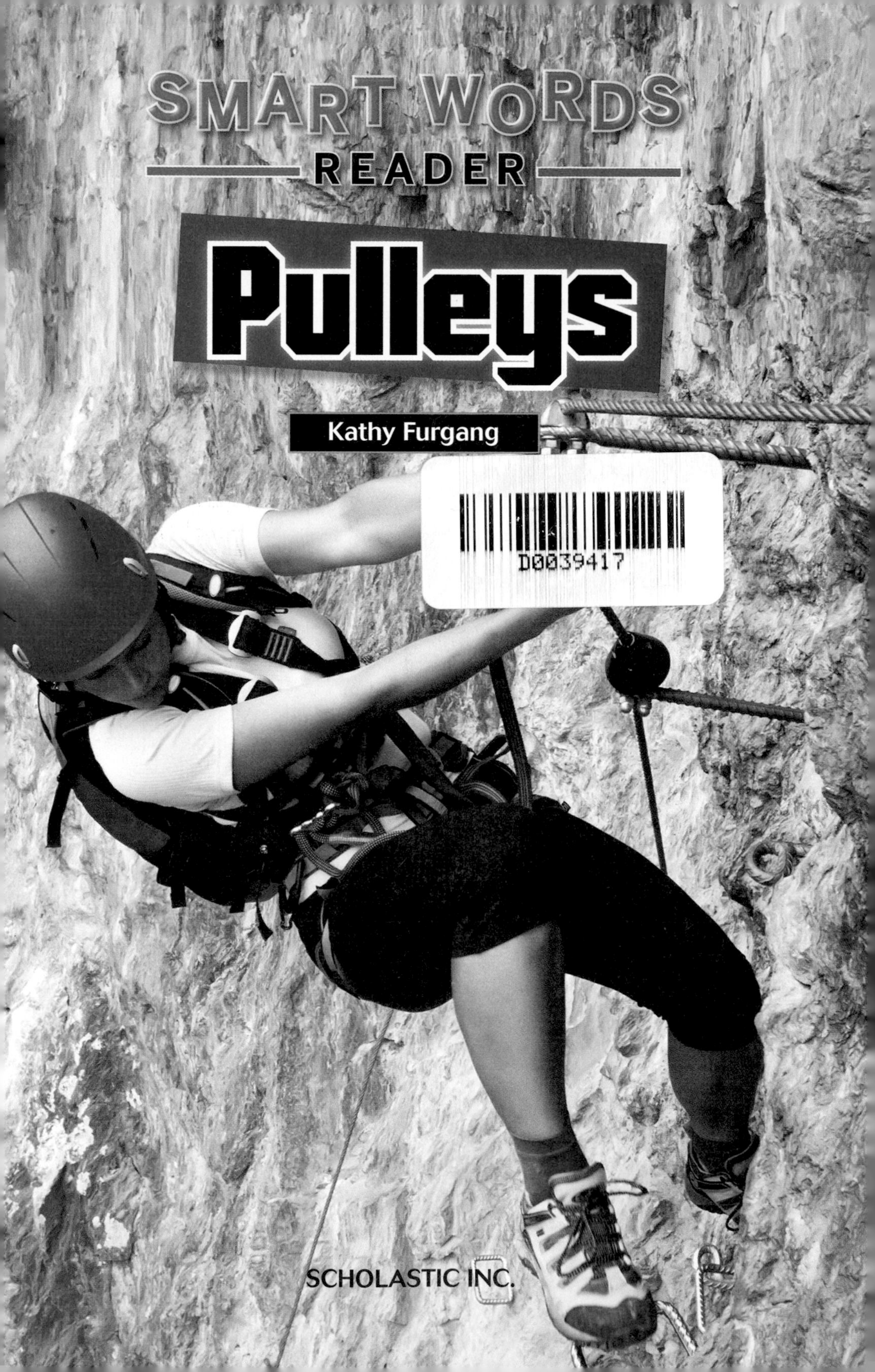
SMART WORDS
READER
Pulleys
Kathy Furgang
D0039417
SCHOLASTIC INC.

What are SMART WORDS?

Smart Words are frequently used words that are critical to understanding concepts taught in the classroom. The more Smart Words a child knows, the more easily he or she will grasp important curriculum concepts. Smart Words Readers introduce these key words in a fun and motivational format while developing important literacy skills. Each new word is highlighted, defined in context, and reviewed. Engaging activities at the end of each chapter allow readers to practice the words they have learned.

ISBN 978-0-545-46708-7

Packaged by Q2A Bill Smith

Series Editor: Barbara M. Linde.

Picture Credit: t= top, b= bottom, l= left, r= right, c= center

Cover Page: Igor Bulgarin/Shutterstock.

Title Page: Jakub Cejpek/Shutterstock.

Content Page: Gregory Epperson/Shutterstock.

4: Gregory Epperson/Shutterstock; 5: Maxim Tupikov/Shutterstock; 6: Andrey Bayda/Shutterstock(cr), Action Sports Photography/Shutterstock(br); 7: Bogdan Ionescu/Shutterstock; 8: Andresr/Shutterstock; 9: Andresr/Shutterstock; 10: Ann Cutting/Botanica/Getty Images; 11: Neil Emmerson/Robert Harding World Imagery/Getty Images; 12: Petr Jilek/Shutterstock; 13: Robert J. Beyers II/Shutterstock; 14: Penka Todorova Vitkova/Shutterstock; 15: Edwin Verin/Shutterstock; 16: Mr. Lightman/Shutterstock; 17: Peter Vahlersvik/iStockphoto; 18: Karnizz/Shutterstock; 19: Craig Cozart/iStockphoto; 20: Catalin Petolea/Shutterstock; 22: Claudia Dewald/iStockphoto; 24: Taylor Hinton/iStockphoto; 27: Maxim Tupikov/Shutterstock; 28: Dragon_fang/Shutterstock; 29: Flashon Studio/Shutterstock.

Q2A Bill Smith Art Bank: 17, 21, 23, 25, 26.

12 11 10 9 8 7 6 5 4 3 2 1 **13 14 15 16 17 18/0**

Printed in the U.S.A. 40

First printing, January 2013

Table of Contents

Chapter 1

Heavy Lifting

Imagine you are climbing a rock cliff, hundreds of feet above the ground. You need a safe way to get yourself and your supplies to the top of the cliff, and back down again, too! Luckily, you have a **simple machine** that can help you to do this. And the simple machine can help to make everything feel lighter and easier to lift. This amazing simple machine is called a **pulley**. Let's find out more about it.

The pulley allows the climber to lift or lower himself and his supplies easily along the face of the rock cliff.

The rope wraps around the wheel and the groove keeps the rope in place.

rope

groove

wheel

A simple machine is a tool with few or no moving parts. A simple machine helps you push, pull, lift, lower, or cut an object.

A pulley is a wheel with a **groove**, or cut, between two raised edges. A rope fits in the groove, and the groove keeps the rope on the wheel.

SMART WORDS

simple machine a tool with few or no moving parts

pulley a simple machine made of a grooved wheel that holds a rope

groove a long, narrow cut in the surface of something

Using the Force

Scientists use the word **force** when they talk about a push or a pull. A pulley changes the direction of a force. When you pull *down* on the rope, the object tied to the rope lifts *up*. The weight of the object being moved is called a **load**.

Look at the sailboat in the picture. The sail is big and heavy. Would you want to climb up the mast to lift the sail? Probably not! Instead, you can use a pulley. The top of the sail is tied to a rope. A pulley at the top of the mast makes the sail easier to lift. You can stand on the deck of the sailboat, pull on the pulley, and watch the sail go up.

A sailboat uses many pulleys to raise and lower the sails.

If any force is added to an object, that object will be set into **motion**. As the rope moves, the **axle**, or center rod, of the wheel allows the pulley to turn around. The rope or the pulley can move. The rope and the wheel and axle must be strong enough to hold the load.

A zip line uses a pulley to move a load from one end of the line to the other. The wheel is above the rope. The wheel, with the load attached below, is in motion along the rope.

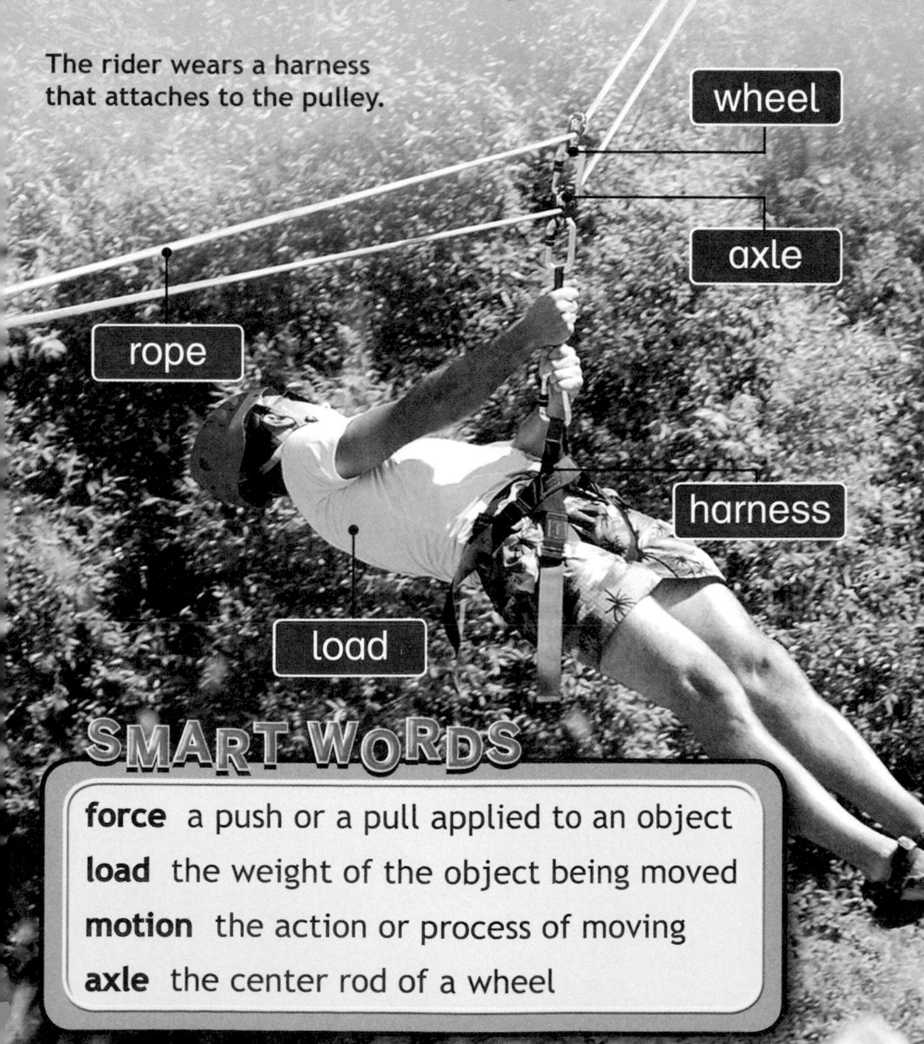

The rider wears a harness that attaches to the pulley.

SMART WORDS

force a push or a pull applied to an object

load the weight of the object being moved

motion the action or process of moving

axle the center rod of a wheel

The pulley on a weight machine may be inside the machine, where you don't see it.

Making the Effort

The force you put on the rope of a pulley is called the **effort**. The effort moves the rope. When the rope moves, the load also moves.

Have you seen or used weight machines like the ones in a gym? These machines use pulleys. The bar is attached to a rope. You use an effort to pull down on the bar. A pulley in the machine changes the direction of the force and the weight lifts up.

Doing Work

When you want to move something over a distance, you apply a force to the object. When the object moves, scientists say that you have done **work**. A simple machine helps make work easier.

Take a look at this exercise machine. If you push on the platform with your legs and it moves, you are doing work. If the platform does not move, no matter how hard you push, you are not doing work.

Is this person doing work? How can you tell?

SMART WORDS

effort the pushing, pulling, or turning force that is made to move something

work applying a force to move something over a distance

Use your SMART WORDS

Match each description to the correct Smart Word.

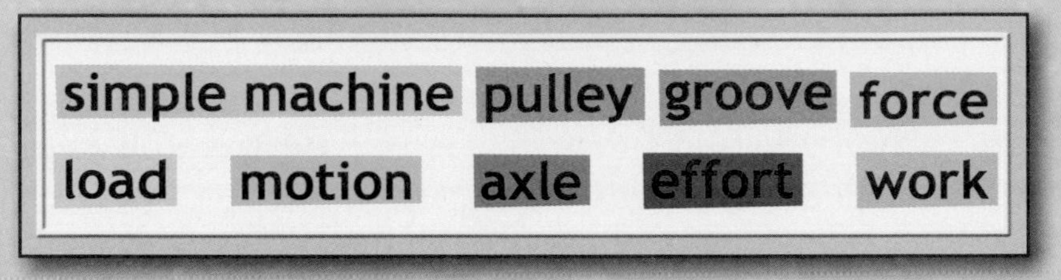

1. the center rod of a wheel
2. applying a force to move an object over a distance
3. a simple machine made of a grooved wheel that holds a rope
4. a push or pull applied to an object
5. the action or process of moving
6. the pushing, pulling, or turning force that is made to move something
7. a tool with few or no moving parts
8. the weight of the object being moved
9. a long, narrow cut in the surface of something

Answers on page 32

Talk Like a Scientist

Your friends want to make a pulley to lift a pail into a tree house. Use your Smart Words to explain what they need to make it and how the pulley will help them do work.

SMART FACTS

Did You Know?

One of the world's tallest ski lifts is at a ski resort in Verbier, Switzerland! The ski lift uses pulleys to lift skiers more than 2 miles (3.2 kilometers) to the top of the ski slopes.

That's Amazing!

Helicopters and huge cranes were needed to get equipment up the mountain to build the ski lift.

Good to Know

The biggest and highest lift at Verbier is the Mont Fort Jumbo lift. This is a cable car that holds up to 150 people!

Chapter 2

Pulleys and More Pulleys

Fixed Pulleys

One type of pulley is called a **fixed pulley**. The wheel of a fixed pulley is attached to an object that does not move, such as a wall, a ceiling, or a pole.

A clothesline attached to a house is a fixed pulley. The pulley stays in one place and the rope moves as the wheel turns. When clothes are attached on the rope, the clothes move, too.

When the top rope moves to the right, the bottom rope moves to the left.

pulley

pulley

right

left

A flagpole uses a fixed pulley. The pulley is attached to the top of the flagpole. The flag is attached to one end of the rope. You pull on the other end of the rope. When you pull, you **hoist** or raise the flag.

This is the simplest kind of pulley because it does not make lifting easier. It only changes the direction of the force. You pull down on the rope and the flag moves up.

When you lower the flag, you push upward on the rope.

SMART WORDS

fixed pulley a pulley that has the wheel attached to an unmoving object

hoist to raise an object with ropes and pulleys

Movable Pulleys

Another kind of pulley is a **movable pulley**. Movable pulleys are able to move along the rope, instead of being fixed in place. The load can then be attached to the pulley as it moves.

A crane uses a movable pulley. A hook attaches the load to the movable pulley. The rope goes around the pulley. When the rope moves, the pulley and the load move.

movable pulley

load

A crane can lift and lower thousands of pounds of material at a time.

With a movable pulley, each side of the rope supports half the weight. That means that half the force is needed to lift the load.

When the effort used with the machine is less than it would be without the machine, we say the machine has a good **mechanical advantage**. A movable pulley has a good mechanical advantage.

SMART WORDS

movable pulley a type of pulley with a wheel that moves with the load

mechanical advantage when a simple machine lets you use less effort to do work

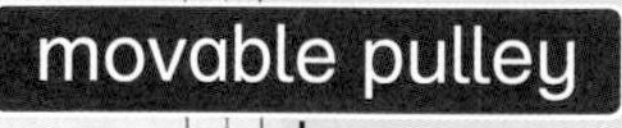

A crane has good mechanical advantage. It can help lift heavy things that you could not lift without it.

moon

Thanks to compound pulleys, you perform your job with ease.

Compound Pulleys

It's helpful that a movable pulley can make an object easier to lift. What happens if more pulleys are added to the first pulley? The object gets even easier to lift and the mechanical advantage is greater. Combining a fixed pulley and a movable pulley makes a **compound pulley**.

Look at the moon in the picture. How can you raise such a heavy prop? Fixed pulleys are attached to the ceiling. Movable pulleys are attached to the load, which is the moon. The compound pulleys solve your problem, and you raise the moon easily.

If you need to lift heavy things, a **block and tackle** is helpful. A block is a set of pulleys on a single axle. A block and tackle is made when a rope is attached to one of the blocks and threaded through both blocks. You pull on the unattached end of the rope. The arrangement of the rope and pulleys allows you to use less effort to move the load. The more pulleys that are used in the blocks, the greater the mechanical advantage. If there are two pulleys, you can lift twice as much weight with the same amount of effort. With more pulleys, you can lift even heavier loads.

The ship's anchor is attached to a block and tackle.

SMART WORDS

compound pulley a fixed pulley and a movable pulley working together

block and tackle sets of pulleys with a single rope that goes around them all and attaches to one set of pulleys

Pulleys for Performers

Imagine watching a show and seeing performers flying through the air. They swoop down and zoom up. You know that people can't fly, so how does this happen? You guessed it — pulleys lift the performers!

The pulleys are attached to the ceiling or to a crane offstage. Performers wear belts or harnesses that attach to the pulleys. Stage workers pull the ropes to lift the performers up and down.

As the ropes of the pulleys are pulled down, the performers are hoisted into the air.

Stage workers on these shows must know about forces and motion. They must know how a load **accelerates**, or speeds up, when it is in motion. They must also know about the way objects slow down. Objects slow down with **friction**, the force of two objects rubbing together.

Stage workers wear gloves because there is friction between their hands and the ropes.

Block-and-tackle pulley systems make the loads easy to control as performers fly through the air.

accelerate to speed up

friction the force of one thing rubbing against another

Use your SMART WORDS

Match each description to the correct Smart Word.

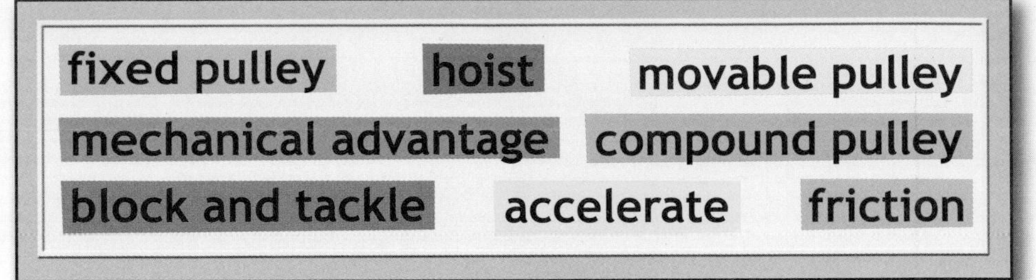

1. This is what happens when a load speeds up.
2. You need to know about this to know how things slow down.
3. This is what you get when a simple machine lets you use less effort to do work.
4. This is a simple machine with a wheel attached to an unmoving object.
5. This is a simple machine with a wheel attached to a moving object.
6. This is a machine made of two types of pulleys.
7. You can arrange pulleys in different ways to make this.
8. This is what happens when something is lifted up with a pulley.

Answers on page 32

Talk Like a Scientist

Show your friend the pulley in the photograph. Use your finger to trace the route of the rope from the pulley to the load. Use Smart Words to describe how the pulley makes work easier.

SMART FACTS

Did You Know?

In 1730, Ben Franklin had a printing press delivered to his printing company, but the machine would not fit up the stairwell to the third floor.

That's Amazing!

Clever Ben solved the problem by making a pulley to lift the printing press up the *outside* of the building instead of the *inside*.

More Great Thinking

Ben Franklin also made a pulley system that allowed him to lock and unlock his bedroom door from his bed.

Chapter 3

Try It Yourself!

Now that you have learned about pulleys, you can use them to have fun! **Investigate** how to send a message using a pulley. You can build your own simple pulleys with common objects around your home. Even just some string and empty spools of thread can help you understand how a pulley works. You don't need everything listed in the activity. Try other objects. You can even use empty toilet-paper rolls instead of spools.

When you investigate, ask an adult for help if you need it. And wear goggles or other safety equipment if necessary. You might want to take photographs, draw pictures, or keep notes as you work.

Write your message on paper or on cardboard.

SMART WORD

investigate to examine something in detail

Send a Message

What You Need
- two empty thread spools
- string
- two pieces of wire
- paper clip
- message

Get Started

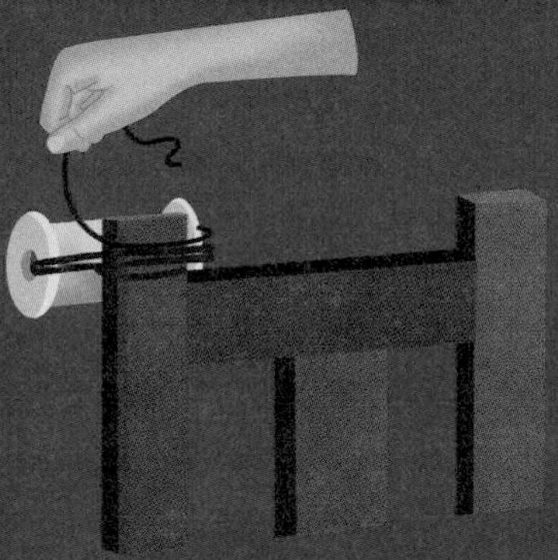

1. Place a wire through each spool of thread. Tie each wire to an unmoving object, such as a bedpost, table leg, or the back of a chair.

2. Wrap and tie the string tightly around the spools as shown. The spools should turn when you move the string.

3. Use the paper clip to attach the message to one end of the string. Move the string to move the message.

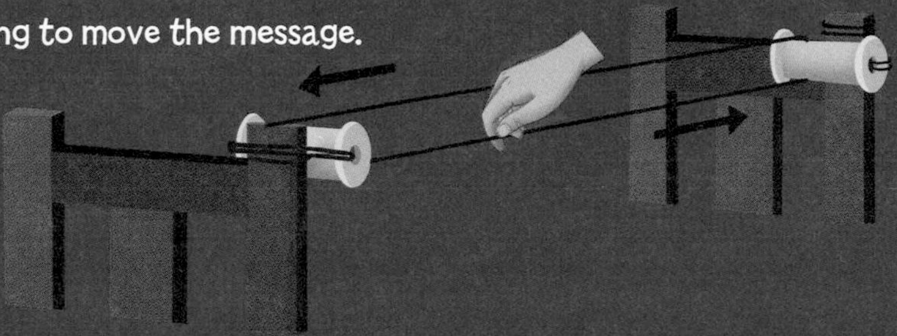

4. Write about how the pulley worked. How can you use the pulley to change the direction that the message moved?

5. How might you improve the design of your next pulley?

Answers on page 32

Don't Get Wet!

Can you make a pulley strong enough to lift a water balloon? What about several water balloons? It will be fun to find out! You can **experiment** to figure out the best way to build a pulley that will hold different loads.

When we experiment in science, we test different ideas to answer a question. In this case, our question might be: *What are the best materials to use to make a pulley that will lift a water balloon?*

Remember, when you add water to the balloon, it becomes heavy! The more water, the heavier the balloon gets.

experiment to test different ideas to answer a question

Get Started

What You Need

- space to work outdoors
- several water balloons
- water
- thin rope
- four or more empty thread spools
- scissors
- masking tape

1. Find an outdoor place to work.
2. Fill the balloons with water. Tie the ends shut.
3. Create a fixed pulley by stringing the rope through a spool and taping the ends of the rope to a support.
4. Run another piece of rope around the pulley, tying one end to a balloon.
5. Try to lift the balloon with the pulley.
6. Did the fixed pulley help? What kinds of pulleys could make this work even easier?

When you build the pulley, think about where the pulley will be attached. The second arrangement makes the load easier to lift.

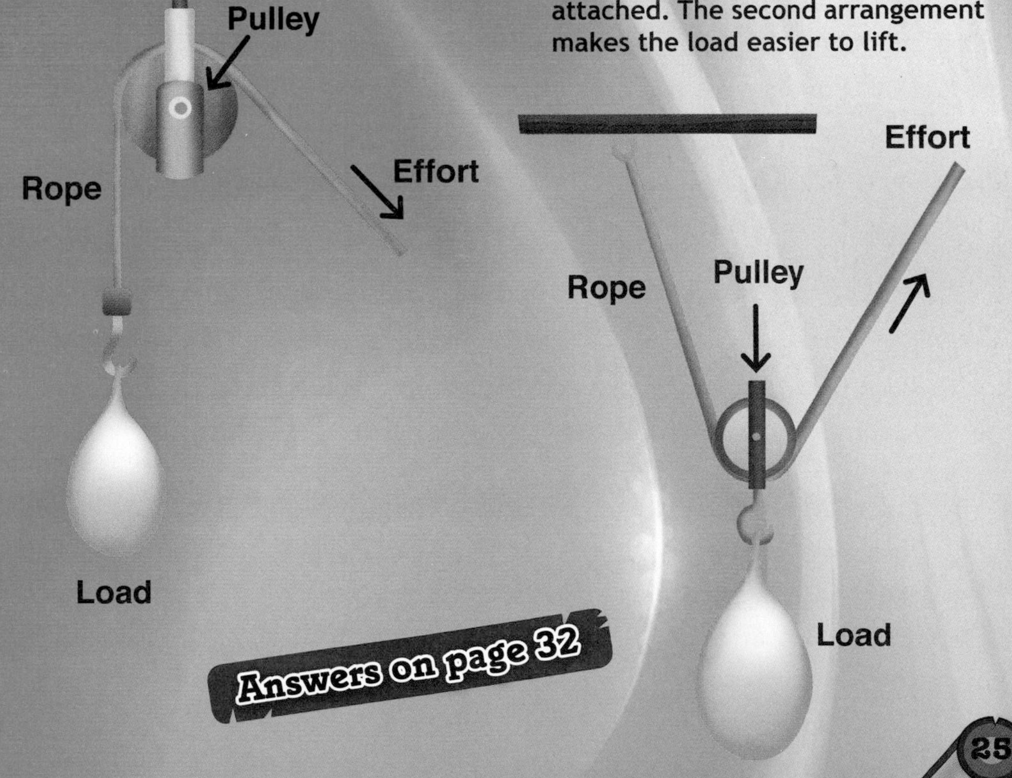

Answers on page 32

Increase Your Strength

Find out how pulleys help you prove you are stronger than two of your friends put together.

What You Need
- two broomsticks
- thin rope
- two friends

Get Started

1. Have each friend hold one broomstick and stand facing each other about two feet apart.

2. Tie one end of the rope around the end of one broomstick handle.

3. Wrap the rope around the broomstick handles three times. Hold the open end of the rope.

4. While your friends stand still, pull slowly on your end of the rope.

5. What happens as you pull on the rope? What happens when you wrap the rope a different number of times?

When you investigate pulleys and other simple machines, you are thinking like an **engineer**. Engineers design and build machines or structures to help people solve problems and do work more easily. Without engineers and their ideas, tests, and experiments, hoisting an anchor, flying across a stage, or climbing a mountain would be much harder — maybe impossible!

The investigations you make about pulleys can help you understand these simple machines better. Take it to the extreme and try out your own tests!

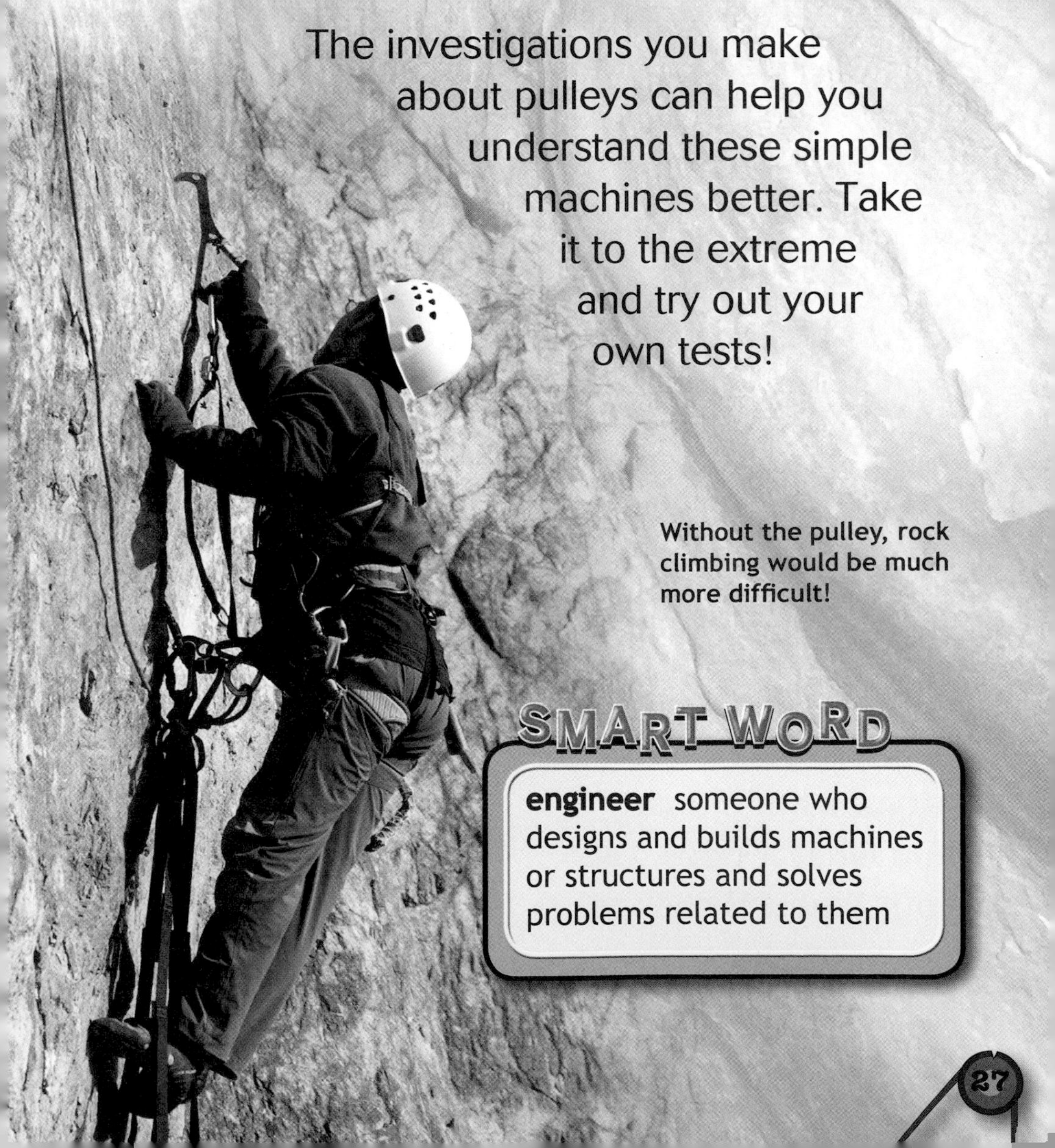

Without the pulley, rock climbing would be much more difficult!

SMART WORD

engineer someone who designs and builds machines or structures and solves problems related to them

Use your SMART WORDS

Read each clue. Choose the Smart Word it describes.

investigate   experiment   engineer

1. This is what happens when you test different ideas to answer a question. You might do this to find the best materials for a certain job.
2. This is someone who designs machines or solves problems related to machines. This person might invent a new gadget to make something easier.
3. This is what you do when you examine something in detail. You might do this to find out how a pulley works.

Answers on page 32

Talk Like a Scientist

You have a friend who has never heard of a pulley. Describe to your friend what a pulley is and what it does. Use your Smart Words to get your ideas across.

SMART FACTS

Did You Know?

Roller coasters like this one use pulleys to move cars up hills and make other parts of the machine move.

How Do They Do It?

Roller coasters hold thousands of pounds of weight and often use pulleys made of metal to hold such large loads.

Good to Know

Some pulleys are often located in the rails of the roller coaster. Other pulleys may be part of the framework.

Glossary

accelerate to speed up

axle the center rod of a wheel

block and tackle sets of pulleys with a single rope that goes around them all and attaches to one set of pulleys

compound pulley a fixed pulley and movable pulley working together

effort the pushing, pulling, or turning force that is made to move something

engineer someone who designs and builds machines or structures and solves problems related to them

experiment to test different ideas to answer a question

fixed pulley a pulley that has the wheel attached to an unmoving object

force a push or a pull applied to an object

friction the force of one thing rubbing against another

groove a long, narrow cut in the surface of something

hoist to raise an object with ropes and pulleys

investigate to examine something in detail

load the weight of the object being moved

mechanical advantage when a simple machine lets you use less effort to do work

motion the action or process of moving

movable pulley a type of pulley with a wheel that moves with the load

pulley a simple machine made of a grooved wheel that holds a rope

simple machine a tool with few or no moving parts

work applying a force to move something over a distance

Index

SMART WORDS Answer Key

Page 10
1. axle, 2. work, 3. pulley, 4. force, 5. motion, 6. effort, 7. simple machine, 8. load, 9. groove

Page 20
1. accelerates, 2. friction, 3. mechanical advantage, 4. fixed pulley, 5. movable pulley, 6. compound pulley, 7. block and tackle, 8. hoist

Page 23
Change the direction of the note by pulling left on one side of the string to make the message move to the right. Designs may be changed by making the pulleys farther apart and sending the message a farther distance.

Page 25
The fixed pulley will help change the direction of your force, but if you really want the work to be easier, try adding more pulleys.

Page 26
When you pull on the rope, the broomsticks act as pulleys, pulling your friends together. The more times the rope is wrapped around the brooms, the easier the job becomes, because the distance the force can travel is increased.

Page 28
1. experiment, 2. engineer, 3. investigate